Chapter 6
The Future

Today, some U.S. leaders believe there is little chance of major wars. They believe there is no need for a large U.S. Navy. As a result, the government has cut some of the navy's funding.

The U.S. Navy has become smaller because of these cuts. But the navy is still strong. It continues to develop stronger and less expensive equipment to defend the United States. This equipment includes new ships and aircraft.

New Warships

The U.S. Navy recently has built new warships like the *Seawolf* and the *Harry S. Truman*. The navy now plans to build new warships. Navy leaders hope these warships will be better and less expensive than today's warships.

The *Seawolf* is one of the navy's newest warships.

New Aircraft

Aircraft play an important role in modern combat. The U.S. Navy is building new and better aircraft to defend the United States and its allies.

The Joint Advanced Strike Technology (JAST) program is building new kinds of aircraft for the navy. The JAST program is building aircraft that can take off from special ramps on aircraft carriers. The navy will be able to launch these aircraft quickly.

New aircraft and warships will help the U.S. Navy remain powerful in the future. The new equipment will help the navy keep the United States safe.

The navy plans to build new and better warships.

WORDS TO KNOW

air strip (AIR STRIP)—a smooth surface where airplanes take off and land

aircraft carrier (AIR-kraft KAIR-ee-ur)—a large warship that carries airplanes

blockade (blok-ADE)—to prevent ships from delivering goods

fleet (FLEET)—a group of warships under one command

hangar (HANG-ur)—a building used to store aircraft

mission (MISH-uhn)—a military task

promote (pruh-MOTE)—to give a higher grade

radar (RAY-dar)—machinery that uses radio waves to locate and guide objects

shipyard (SHIP-yard)—a place where ships are built or repaired

submarine (SUHB-muh-reen)—a warship that can run on the surface of the water or underwater

TO LEARN MORE

Black, Wallace B. *Blockade Runners and Ironclads: Naval Action in the Civil War.* New York: Franklin Watts, 1997.

Green, Michael. *The United States Marines.* Mankato, Minn: Capstone High/Low Books, 1998.

Hole, Dorothy. *The Navy and You.* New York: Crestwood House, 1993.

Streissguth, Thomas. *U.S. Navy SEALs.* Minneapolis: Capstone Press, 1996.

USEFUL ADDRESSES

Intrepid Sea-Air-Space Museum
Pier 86
West 46th Street and 12th Avenue
New York, NY 10036

Naval Historical Center
Washington Navy Yard
901 M Street SE
Washington, DC 20374-5060

Submarine Memorial Museum
P.O. Box 395
Hackensack, NJ 07602

USS Lexington Museum
2914 North Shoreline Boulevard
Corpus Christi, TX 78403-3076

INDY CARS
BY
Scott Robinson

PUBLISHED BY
CRESTWOOD HOUSE
Mankato, MN, U.S.A.

CIP

LIBRARY OF CONGRESS CATALOGING IN PUBLICATION DATA

Robinson, Scott, 1966-
   Indy cars
   (Super-Charged!)
   Includes index.
   SUMMARY: Describes the course and the characteristic features of Formula I cars built
for the Indy 500. Also includes the history of this famous race.
   1. Formula One automobiles — Juvenile literature.   2. Indianapolis Speedway Race —
Juvenile literature.   [1. Formula One automobiles.   2. Indianapolis Speedway Race.   3.
Automobile racing.]   I. Title.
TL236.R563   1988   629.2'28 — dc19   87-30509
ISBN 0-89686-356-5

International Standard
Book Number:
0-89686-356-5

Library of Congress
Catalog Card Number:
87-30509

CREDITS

Cover: Globe Photos, Inc.: (Don L. Black)
Focus West: (Robert Beck) 14, 18, 24-25, 35
UPI/Bettmann Newsphotos: 42-43, 45
Globe Photos, Inc.: (Ken Kaminsky) 12; (Don L. Black) 17, 26, 34; (Toby Rankin) 30-31
Third Coast Stock Source: (Buck Miller) 4-5, 38-39: (Todd V. Phillips) 9, 20-21, 23, 40-41,
   44; (Paul H. Henning) 15, 28-29, 32; (William Meyer) 33
FPG International: (Thomas Zimmerman) 6, 7, 10-11, 37

Produced by Carnival Enterprises.

CRESTWOOD HOUSE

Box 3427, Mankato, MN, U.S.A. 56002

TABLE OF CONTENTS

Thousands of fans gather each year to watch the Indy 500.

INTRODUCTION

Imagine a line of race cars charging down a straight-away at nearly 200 miles per hour (mph) or 320 kilometers per hour (km/h). Engines screaming, the cars are blurs of color as they soar through sharp turns.

Cheers erupt from the excited crowd. The race is on!

Next to horse racing, automobile racing draws the largest crowds of any sport in the world today. Auto racing offers a lot of action for both drivers and fans. The sleek, high-powered racing machines excite all who work on them, drive them, or who simply like to watch them go!

The first formula race car.

THE HISTORY
OF AUTO RACING

Automobile racing has been with us ever since man invented the piston engine. When he bolted it into the frame of a horseless carriage back in the 1880's,

Early racers were larger and slower than today's formula cars.

automobiles were born.

Auto racing grew as automobiles became more plentiful. Early races were usually unplanned. Sometimes they were held just so racers could show off their cars—and their cars' speed. As automobiles became faster and more powerful, there were more serious accidents. People were upset over the wildness in the streets and demanded that drivers organize their races.

The Europeans were the first to organize auto racing in the early 1900's. An association called the Federation Internationale de l'Automobile (FIA) was formed in Paris, France, in 1904. The FIA set up rules of competition for races, track standards, driver qualifications, and prizes. The FIA still rules over international competition, and its regulations have been adopted throughout the world.

In the United States, fairground horse tracks were usually modified to handle auto races. Facilities expanded, the public grew more interested, and the popularity of auto racing surged.

THE INDIANAPOLIS MOTOR SPEEDWAY

Indianapolis, Indiana, businessman Carol G. Fisher and three of his friends had a dream. In 1908, they put their money together and began to build what they thought of as a "great outdoor laboratory" for automobiles. They wanted to provide a place where automobiles and auto parts manufacturers could test their products safely, under controlled conditions. This outdoor lab also featured a track designed especially for auto racing.

A crew member clocks a racer in an Indy time trial.

The first Indianapolis race was not just one race, but a series of races: car against car, car against the time clock, and motorcycle against motorcycle.

Three days of events were scheduled with the major event to be a 300-mile (480 km/h) auto race on the final day. Even before the race started, it was obvious that the crushed rock and tar road surface had taken a beating from the other events. With 17 cars pounding the surface in the final race, the track began to crumble. Officials stopped the race at 235 miles (380 kilometers) because the course conditions had become too dangerous.

The Indianapolis Speedway or "Brickyard" as it looks today.

Fisher and his associates immediately decided they would need the strongest track surface available. After making some tests, they decided on bricks, which would be laid in cement. Nothing could be stronger

INTERNET SITES

The Big Mamie Home Page
http://www.ici.net/cust_pages/jack/mamie.html

U.S. Navy History
http://www.history.navy.mil

**United States Naval & Shipbuilding
  Museum Online**
http://www.uss-salem.org/

U.S. Navy: Welcome Aboard
http://www.navy.mil/

USS Kitty Hawk
http://trout.nosc.mil/~cv63pao/

INDEX

than that! The bricks gave the track its nickname: the "Brickyard." Today, even though the track is now paved and there are no longer any bricks, the track still keeps its old nickname.

In the summer of 1910, racing events were held on Memorial Day, Fourth of July, and Labor Day weekends, but attendance was low. Fisher met with auto manufacturers, race drivers, and his partners. They decided that instead of sponsoring a series of events, they would have one event—the biggest in

Formula I cars are fast!

racing! The race would cover 500 miles (800 kilometers). This distance would subject cars and drivers to the most grueling punishment. To attract newspaper interest, the track announced that it would award a first prize of $25,000.

On Memorial Day, 1911, the first official Indianapolis 500 was run. Six hours, 42 minutes, and 8 seconds after the starter's flag had dropped, Ray Harroun crossed the finish line. He had clocked a dazzling speed of 74.59 mph (120 km/h) to win the prize money. The crowds, the fame, and the prize money at Indianapolis have grown ever since that race in 1911.

GRAND PRIX RACING

The oldest race held outside of the United States is the very popular Grand Prix. Grand Prix means "Big Prize" in French.

There are more than a dozen kinds of Grand Prix racing, each called a "Formula." Formula 1 is the most glamorous and dangerous form of auto racing. Formula 1 racing cars are designed and built only for the "Grand Prix, Formula 1 Circuit," which includes an international schedule of events leading to a world championship. The most famous of all Grand Prix races is the one held on the steets of Monaco, on the French Riviera.

A wedge-shaped formula car.

FORMULA RACING CARS

Some formula cars are wedge-shaped, while others look like giant doorstops or even low-slung bathtubs on wheels! A Formula 1 racing car is one with a large body carrying a name like Lotus, Eagle, Mongoose, or Coyote. The engine, which is generally located behind the driver, is often built by Ford, Offenhauser, or Chevrolet. The finished racing machine often has a

The engine of a formula car is located behind the driver.

name that reflects its well-bred heritage: Lotus-Ford, Eagle-Offenhauser, or another combination.

Some formula cars are highly specialized for race track driving. These cars can drive fast and straight on speedways like Indianapolis, Pocono, and Ontario. The races on these tracks are always run counterclockwise. This means a driver is always being pushed to the right, inside his tight cockpit, through every single turn. The driver is protected from this constant, bruising pressure by extra padding on the right side of the cockpit. Also, the strength of the tires, the wheel suspension, and the fuel distribution are designed to meet the extra demands made on the right side of the car.

Most Formula 1 cars are lightweight and are highly maneuverable. Since these qualities help on paved ovals as well as road courses, many formula cars have been modified for track racing too.

INDY 500 CARS

Indy cars are the most sophisticated Formula I cars in the racing industry. Big and powerful, their turbo-charged engines are able to generate over 700 horsepower. A large family sedan can generate only 350 horsepower, yet a family car weighs nearly twice as much as a 1,350-pound (612 kilograms) Indy car. This combination of great power and light weight makes Indy cars fleet and sensitive to drive.

A turbo-charged engine makes use of its own exhaust to drive a special fan. This fan sucks extra air into the engine to aid combustion and add power. A championship racer, as Indy cars are often called, can accelerate and dodge like a rabbit, producing an average speed of more than 170 mph (270 km/h) on a large oval track.

An Indy turbo-charged engine is powerful.

Because of their special design, championship cars are not suitable for other types of racing. They burn powerful fuel mixtures containing alcohol or nitromethane instead of ordinary gasoline. Such a hot fuel concoction adds extra horsepower to the racer, but it cuts mileage and is hard on the engine.

Indy cars usually have a three-speed transmission, while road racers have a four- or five-speed transmission. The driver only uses the first two gears during starts and after pit stops. The rest of the race is

Brightly-colored formula cars round a turn at high speeds.

18

run in high gear. The driver controls his speed with the throttle and brakes.

Indy cars are one-purpose vehicles, custom-built to run the 500. Owners, however, can make adjustments to enable the car to run other kinds of races. They can drop in a new engine. They can change the suspension for better traction so the springs and shocks will take the uneven jolts of a road course. They can change the gear box and put on different tires. In other words, owners can make their cars fit the formula for any race!

BRAKES

For an Indy Car, the brakes are as important as the engine. This seems strange in a sport where the object is speed! But on a speedway like Indy, high speeds are strictly for the straightaways. Brakes are necessary for the tight turns. Brakes slow or stop a car by pushing pads against the wheels to slow their rotation. This friction causes the brake pads to get extremely hot.

There are two types of brakes used on most cars: drum and disc. Today, the most common brake used is the disc brake. This braking system is less affected by the heat that friction causes. It is also unaffected by mud and water. This makes disc brakes ideal for racing, where braking is critical.

Wrenches inspect the race car of driver Michael Andretti.

21

SUSPENSION

The Indy car's suspension is a key factor in racing performance. Professional drivers say that a car must "handle" well. Good handling depends on proper weight distribution and responsive steering. But the most important factor is the car's suspension.

A car touches the road at just four points—the wheels. Everything else in the car is suspended from those wheels. A car's suspension means the way the rest of the car is connected to the axle and wheels.

One type of suspension is considered best. All modern racing cars have independent front-wheel suspension. Independent suspension allows a left wheel to remain unaffected while a right wheel goes over bumps. One wheel stays on the ground even when the opposite wheel is up in the air. Independent suspension is a great way for the Indy car to tame a rough race track!

BODY AND FRAME

The body of an Indy car is made of steel, light metal, or fiberglass. Fiberglass is much lighter than steel, but it is very expensive. And, unlike metal, fiberglass has

Driver Dan Sullivan's Indy car.

Streamlining helps Indy cars operate at their best.

a tendency to crack and break rather than bend. Minor repairs are easy with fiberglass, but major ones are difficult.

Streamlining a car is just as important as making the race car light. Streamlining means smoothing the

shape of the body and frame. At high speeds, wind resistance can reduce times and threaten overall performance. By streamlining both the body and underside of a car, wind resistance is cut. A car's top speed will be improved. And that can win the race!

Before a race, a wrench works on an Indy car in the pit.

COCKPIT AND INSTRUMENTS

The cockpit of an Indy car should be comfortable so the driver can concentrate on his driving. The bucket seat helps by holding the driver firmly in position during sharp turns. The safety belt helps the driver stay in a comfortable driving position.

The most important instrument in the cockpit is the tachometer. It shows the speed at which the engine is turning and is a *must* for racing. The tachometer is large and easy to read at a glance. The speedometer, however, is rarely used. A race car driver is not interested in his speed. He's more concerned with how efficient his engine is performing.

The second most important instrument in the cockpit is the oil pressure gauge. This tells the driver whether oil is being pushed to all parts of the engine at the right pressure. A drop in oil pressure is the first sign that an engine is in trouble.

The water and oil temperature gauges rank next in importance. These tell the driver if his engine is overheating. A charge indicator is also in the cockpit to tell the driver about the electrical system.

THE MECHANICS

A professional race car driver would be lost without his garage mechanics. The cars are cared for by a chief mechanic, aided by a small group of "wrenches," as mechanics are often called.

In the Indy 500, getting the car set for a race is the chief mechanic's job. He oversees everything that goes on in the garage and in the pits. In addition to his salary, the chief wrench gets a percentage of any winnings earned by the driver.

In the dark early morning hours before the Indy 500 race, an amazing amount of work remains to be done.

A fast pit crew is an important part of a winning race team.

The pit crew selects the proper tires for the day's race.

In its own pit space, an Indy racer is up on blocks, with all wheels removed and the entire body standing in a corner. The mechanics will have to put all parts of the car together and go through a weigh-in and technical inspection before the race deadline.

Mechanics drop a new engine into a chassis and

begin connecting wires and rods. While this is being done, the chief mechanic studies track conditions very closely to see which tires he should put on the car. He has the basic choices of wet, dry, or intermediate tires, each using a different kind of rubber. Proper tires are as important as a well-tuned engine for racing success.

Wrenches put last-minute touches on a racer's car.

In time, the wrenches have the car properly set up. Engine, gears, suspension, and weight distribution are in tune with each other. If anything is out of balance, the car will perform poorly. Now if something goes wrong, the mechanics will say it's a faulty "Johnson Rod." A Johnson Rod is the made-up part racing people blame when things go wrong!

At this point the chief mechanic fires up the engine and assists the driver. Before leaving the pit area, a

A good helmet is needed to protect drivers in case of a crash.

check is made of all safety equipment. The crew checks
the fire extinguisher that is required in every car. The
fire-resistant driving suit is inspected, from tight cuffs
and collar to zippers and fasteners. The crash helmet
is adjusted for comfort as well as safety. A new five-
layer plastic face shield is set in place. During the race,
oil or dirt can splatter and obscure the driver's vision.
When that happens, he can reach up and pull off the
top layer of the face shield!

A formula car is moved into the pit area.

PIT STOPS

Indy and other speedways have an area where cars are serviced between racing laps. That area is called the pit. Indy's pit area stretches along the main straightaway. It is separated from the track by a low concrete wall. The road leading into the pit branches off the main speedway after the final turn before reaching the start/finish line.

The pit crew works quickly to get the Indy car back into the race.

The pits themselves are simple, marked-off numbered parking spaces behind the guard wall. Each driver has his own pit space and his own crew. Before each race, the drivers and their pit crews load their space with spare parts, tools, tires, and fuel storage tanks—everything to keep their driver's car racing!

Generally, a limited number of crew members are allowed in the pit during a pit stop. To eliminate danger and confusion, any additional wrenches must do their jobs from behind the pit wall. An engine expert may lean over to listen to the engine. Another crew member may put a cold drink on the end of a stick and pass it to the driver. Still another at the fuel storage tank will stand behind the wall and control the liquid flowing through hoses to the racer's tanks.

TIME TRIALS

The track at Indianapolis Motor Speedway is not wide enough for all cars to start the race side-by-side. This means that some racers have to start behind others. This gives the drivers near the front a slight advantage over those near the rear of the pack. A car's location at the start of the race is called its "pole position." The driver with the Number 1 pole position is the driver in the first row, closest to the inside of the track.

To be fair, trials are held the week before the big race to determine who gets the best pole positions. Drivers speed around the track a number of laps by themselves. After several days of trials, the driver with the fastest speed and time is awarded the top pole position. The driver with the second-fastest time is awarded the Number 2 position, and so forth.

An Indy racer leans into the turn.

"DRIVERS, START YOUR ENGINES!"

The day of the Indy 500 arrives Memorial Day Weekend. Thousands from all over the country arrive to fill the grandstand and the infield to watch the most famous race in the United States.

Finally, the bright-colored cars move onto the Brickyard. The drivers take their pole positions. The cars stretch back the length of the straightaway. The

Indy cars head down the straightaway.

pace car leads the procession of Indy cars once around the track. The pace car speeds up to bring the racers faster and faster around the oval track.

As the pack of racers passes the grandstand, a race official on a high platform above the starting line waves a green flag. The engines roar. The race is on!

A car fuels-up before the Indy 500.

A formula car slides sideways and causes problems for other drivers.

THE WINNER'S CIRCLE

During the race, some cars will give out. Busted fuel lines, overheated engines, and broken throttles will force more than a few drivers into the pit area. They are out of the race until next year. Sometimes cars spin out of control to avoid a crash. Usually, they can't recover the momentum they'll need to catch up with

the front-runners.

As they near the end, drivers search for that extra energy that will keep their cars in the race just one more lap. They round Turn Number 4 — the final turn. One car is just seconds ahead of another. The car in front zooms past the grandstand and across the finish line as the official waves the checkered flag. The winner!

The Indy 500 Winner's Trophy.

Driver Al Unser celebrates in the Winner's Circle after his fourth Indy 500 win.

Directly behind the pit area is the Winner's Circle. Here, the winner of the Indy 500 receives the trophy! The Winner's Circle is really a ramp that is tilted toward the grandstand. The winner is in full view of spectators and television cameras. When a driver is brought into the Winner's Circle, he is met with applause and instant fame. The other drivers all begin to talk about next year. Another Indy 500 is already underway!

GLOSSARY/INDEX

ACCELERATE 16 — *To increase the speed of a vehicle.*

AXLE 22 — *The shaft that connects the wheels of a vehicle and allows them to turn. One axle connects the two front wheels and one connects the back wheels.*

BRICKYARD 11, 37 — *The nickname given to the race track at the Indianapolis Motor Speedway.*

CHASSIS 30 — *The framework that supports the body and engine of a vehicle.*

COCKPIT 15, 16, 26, 27 — *The driver's seat.*

DISC BRAKES 19 — *A braking system that consists of one metal disc revolving with each wheel. A pair of rods presses against the wheel and metal disc during braking.*

FORMULA 1 CAR 13, 14, 15, 16 — *Highly specialized racing cars designed and built for the Grand Prix, Formula 1 racing circuit.*

HORSEPOWER 16, 17 — *The unit for measuring the power of an engine.*

INDY CAR 16, 17, 19, 22, 26, 38 — *A type of Formula 1 car built especially for the Indianapolis 500 race.*

PIT 17, 27, 30, 32, 34, 35, 36, 42, 45 — *The area where cars are refueled, serviced, and repaired (if possible) during the race.*

POLE POSITION 36, 37 — *A car's position on the track at the start of a race.*

SPEEDOMETER 27 — *The instrument in a driver's cockpit that shows how fast the vehicle is traveling.*

GLOSSARY/INDEX

STREAMLINING 24, 25 — *To smooth the body and frame of a racing car to allow the airflow to pass around the vehicle without slowing it down.*

SUSPENSION 16, 19, 22, 32 — *The components that connect the chassis of a vehicle to the axles.*

TACHOMETER 26, 27 — *The instrument that tells the driver how fast the car engine is turning over.*

TURBO-CHARGED ENGINE 16 — *An engine that receives extra power from steam, water, or air.*

WRENCH 27, 32, 35 — *The nickname for mechanics.*